Strengthen

What Remains

Daily Motivation For The Believer That Refused To Give Up

Eddie Parker IV

— To Jordan
I Pray This Helps Your
Already Dope Journey

Strengthen What Remains

Daily Motivation For The Believer That Refused
To Give Up

ISBN ISBN-13: 978-1546642527

ISBN-10: 1546642528

For booking inquiries or permissions e-mail
eddie.tyes@gmail.com

Foreword

Cornelius Lindsey
Founder and Senior Pastor,
The Gathering Oasis Church

I've had many guys approach me asking what should they do to change. However, I've only had a few to rise to the occasion and excel beyond their limitations. I have seen Eddie bounce back from many difficult situations. His unwillingness to quit and succumb to normal is both encouraging and enlightening. From our first conversation, I knew his faith was strong and his will was resolute. It has been exciting to watch his development and growth right before my eyes.

I am convinced that great men are those who choose to empower their peers and the next generation. They consider what's to come and work hard to bringing influence and change to their community. Eddie and I have conversed about his ability for quite a while now, and this is another reason why I am so excited to endorse him as he takes a step of faith to empower the masses with the words in this book.

You will be inspired and encouraged by what you read in this book. Approach each page with an open mind and a desire to change. I am convinced that you will read something that will change your life forever. You will develop a resilience to keep going, and you will apply this practical message of hope. You are a winner through Jesus Christ, and you can use what He has given you to complete the journey He has for you. Christ Strengthens What Remains so you are able finish what He has given you to complete.

Be encouraged.

Dedication

This book is a tribute to the legacy of powerful men that stand before me: My grandpa, Eddie Parker Jr. and my Dad, Eddie Parker III. This book exists because of the wisdom you have imparted. The odds have always been stacked but somehow we've managed to overcome.

To Eddie V (EJ) my son, may the legacy continue.

TABLE OF
CONTENTS

Preface

I'll be the first to admit my story is far from perfect. Imagine the typical loving, strong 90's sitcom mom and the disciplined, hardworking sitcom dad, those are my amazing parents in a nutshell. Married forever, they taught balance and the importance of God in our lives. You would think that would've given me a fail proof plan to conquer life, wrong! I have fought with bipolar behavior, experienced divorce and struggled with negative self-medicating, proving that life plays no favorites but things could've been worse. All of these life moments have combined to create a stronger me, more refined by my pursuit to inspire those who have dealt with the same or worse. I was able to overcome, rebuild, revive and recover. Everything we experience in life makes it possible for us to share our story and connect with people that will stand beside us and declare, "we're stronger than we realize".

This book was birthed by the things that were supposed to kill me. Guess what? I guess it worked.....together....for my good!!!!!

Intro

As humans, we're blessed with this uncanny ability to bounce back from the most difficult situations. This resounding resilience fueled by faith, gives us the confidence to believe that difficulties in life are just detours in our journey.

Daily we're blessed with a fresh dose of grace that provides protection and offers forgiveness, undeserved but vital to the recovery process.

One of the many things I love about The Bible is that it packs so many practical lessons that answer some of life's most complex situations. Isn't it amazing that a book written over 2,000+ years ago still has relevance today? So with that as a starting point, I have extracted 21 simple yet powerful principles into the pages of this book to push you to strengthen every facet of your life by referencing the oldest self-help book ever written "The Bible".

Here's the game plan that changed it all for me. Start the day unplugged from distraction i.e social media and begin the day with talking to God (prayer time), daily reading and a Strength Statement (a positive affirmation declaring good). Sometimes the smallest steps in the right direction can make the biggest impact. Be consistent. Real growth and development take time and lasting change takes discipline. Trust me.

You'll begin to see strengthening processes at work before you know it. I want to present this practical message of hope, "just because you lose in life doesn't mean you've lost". I am a firm believer that we can be restored and reminded of our true potential.

Strengthen What Remains is for the believer who refused to give up.

Today is the first day of your brand new journey and I am so excited about the transformations that will happen over the next 30 days. Congratulations! Welcome to

#ProjectStrength

RE·STORE

/rə'stôr/

"And the God of all grace, who called you to his eternal glory in Christ, after you have suffered a little while, will himself restore you and make you strong, firm and steadfast."
−1 Peter 5:10 NIV

It seems crazy to see potential in something others consider useless right? Most people don't have enough patience to see the value in damaged things anymore.

The one thing I've always admired was the restoration of old homes and vintage collectables. They usually come slightly damage and often discarded. Although new and modern is appealing, there is something compelling about an item that has been handpicked, reclaimed and admired not by its current state but the possibility of its potential.

Life can beat us up, damaged our confidence and narrow our perspective. But God, The ultimate designer, still sees our purpose. He loves to take the least and last and use them for His glory.

Allow your life to be a testimony of restoration. Give it time. Give Him the broken pieces of your life and watch Him turn it in a masterpiece.

Strength Statement

The broken pieces of my life still have purpose. The scars will heal and my faith will be restored.

MORNING

MOTIVATION

HAVE ENOUGH **FAITH** TO LET YOUR
BIGGEST DISAPPOINTMENTS
REROUTE NOT RUIN YOUR
DIRECTION.

DE•CLARE

/di'kler

"Thou shalt also decree a thing, and it shall be established unto thee: and the light shall shine upon thy ways."

-Job 22:28

Words have power. I love the quote by Yehuda Berg that says, "Words are singularly the most powerful force available to humanity. We can choose to use this force constructively with words of encouragement, or destructively using words of despair. Words have energy and power with the ability to help, to heal, to hinder, to hurt, to harm, to humiliate and to humble."

Purposefully constructed words can

change our perception of reality. Media overwhelmingly promotes words used to tear down, criticize and degrade, but there is another way. You have the ability to refuse what mainstream culture tries to convince us is normal, become a voice of peace and let your words uplift, inspire and cultivate change in the people around you.

When Jesus spoke; things changed. The sick were healed and the dead came back to life. The same power lives in us today. Jesus says we have the power to move mountains with our words (anything that stands before us that seems impossible).

Our words + Faith = Change

Strength Statement

I Speak Life, because I know my words were heard, and He will come in response to them.

SEA•SONS

/see-zuh n/

"And he said unto them, It is not for you to know the times or the seasons, which the Father hath put in his own power."

- Acts 1:7

Life is made up of a series of seasons (moments and experiences). It's a proven fact that the earth's distance to the sun dictates its seasons and I'm convinced that our proximity to the Son will dictate ours.

The entire nature of a "season" indicates that regardless of its length, it has to end. It comes only to serve a temporary assignment.

There's good news for stormy conditions. The severity of the storm will never change its assignment. Its come to pass.

You must make a conscious effort to remain faithful in every season. Think about it. You wouldn't appreciate those crisp spring mornings as much if you weren't just coming out of the blistering cold of winter. Learn to enjoy every season because complaining causes you to miss the joy of the journey.

Take a moment today to write down a few things the current season in your life has taught you.

Strength Statement

I'm as strong on the bad days as I am on the good because Seasons change but My God never does.

GRO•WTH

/grōTH/

"Instead, speaking the truth in love, we will grow to become in every respect the mature body of him who is the head, that is, Christ."

-Ephesians 4:15

Growing pains hurt. As a kid, there was nothing worse than waking up in the middle of the night with that unconformable pain throbbing down my legs. It wasn't until later in life that I discovered that the pain I felt wasn't actually connected to the growth process. Although they're called growing pains, they are actually caused by a lower pain threshold. There's no evidence to suggest that growth hurts.

Yes, growth is necessary for the body

and minds to expand its capacity, but not everything you think are growing pains are actually associated with your growing process.

This got me thinking; many times the wrong people at the wrong times in our life can bring us pain and we're so blinded by how good it looks and feels on the outside that we fail to realize they are slowing our development.

It is important for us to take inventory of the things in our lives and make sure that we are doing everything we can to facilitate positive growth.

Make a conscious decision to develop growth-generating actions and surround yourself with people that push you to be better. Cut out toxic relationships, talk to God more, find an accountability partner, push beyond what's been done and seen.

Real Growth Leaves Evidence

Strength Statement

Increase my capacity for You! Make me into the better and more complete person that I need to be. Make me more like Jesus every day, mind, body, heart and spirit.

WAKE•UP!

/'wākəp/

"And do this, understanding the present time: The hour has already come for you to wake up from your slumber, because our salvation is nearer now than when we first believed."

-Romans 13:11 NIV

On my twenty-sixth birthday I received a very interesting message that would change my life forever. The message came from a close family friend and mentor. After thanking him for the birthday wishes he replied, "You are welcome...new life begins today...don't let any moss grow under your feet...don't lose years...take care of your business fast...decide what you need and want to do and get it!! A nation is depending on you, don't mess it up...it's on you Rev...write a book, and develop a message/sermon...do it quick!!"....Little did he know this was the exact wakeup call I needed.

Think about it. We all have experienced that "ahh-ha moment" that has the ability to move us to a level of conscious that reveals there's work to be done. It's extremely important to harness that new clarity and maximize the moment.

The period after failure is a space I like to call a pregnant moment. Every subsequent choice thereafter can make or break your destiny.

Today is the day you take action,
consider yourself woke and prime to
live out your dreams

I've seen so many talented, creative
and brilliant minds go to waste because
they were okay with being inactive in
the areas where God has called them to
excel.

Don' let your Dreams stay Dreams
forever.

Strength Statement

I will maximize the moment, I will be more conscious of Your voice. Today's the day to wake up, level up, and keep moving

AD·VANCE

əd'vans/

"Be diligent in these matters; give yourself wholly to them, so that everyone may see your progress."
-1 Timothy 4:15

Progress is a unique idea because often times our definition varies by interpretation.

Sometimes we get stuck with the notion that just because we don't see instant results that moment, it isn't taking place. When you plant a seed in the ground, it takes some time before we see its fruit. Most people only consider your positive movement to be a visible movement but only you know that the majority of the blood, sweat, and tears happened behind the scenes.

We can advance our dreams in many ways. These ways include: a course you decide to pick up to polish your craft, a sermon on success you choose to listen to, a few dollars you set aside weekly to invest into your ideas. As long as we are doing something, no matter how little, to bring our dreams to life, then we are making progress.

We hear this expression all the time. "Rome wasn't built in a day". Although, I tend to shy away from clichés, this concept is profoundly simple but simply profound. Stop beating yourself up because you feel you are not taking giant strides or moving forward in leaps and bounds. We build our lives in stages laying one brick of positive action after another. Celebrate your small victories and pursue the next challenge with more faith than the last.

Strength Statement

I'll continue to work for it while I wait for it.

PUR•POSE

/'pər-pəs/

MORNING

MOTIVATION

GOD **WONT** STOP, WHAT HE STARTS
UNTIL HE'S **FINISHED.**

"But I have raised you up for this very purpose, that I might show you my power and that my name might be proclaimed in all the earth"

-Exodus 9:16

Everything that exists was created for a purpose. God has placed purpose in each and every one of us. One of life's greatest questions illuminates this idea. "Why am I here". May I humbly suggest that you are here to make a difference, to create, invent, impact and succeed. You were made by God and equipped with a unique set of skills and abilities which, when unleashed in the right moment and under the right conditions, will change your life and the lives of those around you. Perhaps even the entire world. In order for you to find purpose, we must give our life's plans over to God and be ready to accept His will. This might seem scary, but God has only good things in mind for you. He created you. Of all the things that God created, we were the only things he put his hands on. Believe me; knowing why you are on this earth is one of the most liberating and empowering things that can happen to anyone. It frees you from envy and jealousy because you know that there is room for everyone to succeed in their own lane.

It's normal to feel like, "yeah I already found my purpose, but life has dealt me a blow of sickness, loss, failure. There's no way I can fulfill it anymore."

Well, it is people like you that God loves to use! He loves to take the forgotten people of this world and use them to do great things.

Let me be clear about something. The enemy isn't concerned about people with no purpose. So it's important for us to strengthen the weak areas of our lives to protect what God has so masterfully placed in us. Life without purpose is a paralyzing process. You are relevant! Discover your purpose and develop your plan.

MORNING

MOTIVATION

IN A WORLD WITH SO MUCH
CLUTTER & NOISE
WE MUST ACTIVELY CREATE SPACE
TO HEAR **GODS** VOICE

OUCH!

ouCH/

"For I consider that the sufferings of this present time are not worth comparing with the glory that is to be revealed to us."
-Romans 8:18

Our pain is one of the best ways our body identifies problems. The ability to feel pain, whether physical or emotional, keeps us aware of harmful situations. You rarely have to tell a kid not to stick their finger in the socket twice; more often than not, they learned that the feeling associated with the act was something they don't want to experience again.

Although temporarily uncomfortable, the absence of pain is the absence of life. The moment that we become numb to it, we start to make critical decisions without considering the consequences.

Embrace the pain and focus on what is waiting for you on the other side. Feelings are good, healthy in fact, but allow them to push you towards results not a pity parade.

Dealing with our scars from past pains can be unpleasant but scars are proof that wounds heal. The only way we can effectively strengthen any area of our lives is by addressing that discomfort directly

The fact that your idea or a relationship failed doesn't mean that the entire venture was a bust. Maybe the timing was off and maybe it was a lack perpetration or commitment.

The pain of failure can haunt you if you let it but I've learned to use it as a tool so the pain I am experiencing now is my indicator that something in my life needs to change. Make more effort, less excuses or create new surroundings. Let your discomfort lead you to your deliverance.

MORNING

MOTIVATION

LET YOUR **PURPOSE** CHANGE YOU
YOUR CIRCLE
THEN LET IT CHANGE THE WORLD.

AVE·RAGE

\\\'a-v(ə-)rij\\

"But you are a chosen people, a royal priesthood, a holy nation, God's special possession, that you may declare the praises of him who called you out of darkness into his wonderful light."
- 1 Peter 2:9

We have to make the choice daily not to let the mediocrity of others be the norm for us. The Bible is FULL of people who refused to focus on their inability and chose to believe in God's ability working through them.
[you can too]
We as believers we're designed to step out of the dark shadows of conformity and shine bright with God ordained confidence. We're called to be agents

of change and examples of God's amazing love. There's nothing average about that. What God is calling you to do may seem unusual considering your current situations but inside each ounce of faith are above average seeds capable to move mountains.

The land of mediocrity is a toxic place for any dreamer to live. Ideas get lost and visions get buried. But from today on, no more living in the darkness of ordinary thinking when God has called us into his marvelous light. It's time to shine. Don't follow the crowd, follow the King!

Strength Statement

Today I will challenge the status quo, push innovation and refuse to be average. I will not be afraid to do it differently!

MID•NIGHT

/'mid₁nīt/

MORNING

MOTIVATION

DEAR JESUS

I'M SORRY FOR THE TIMES I THOUGHT
YOU WOULDN'T COME THROUGH. HELP ME
BELIEVE THAT WHAT I'M **LEARNING**
OUTWEIGHS WHAT I'VE
LOST.

"About midnight Paul and Silas were praying and singing hymns to God, and the prisoners were listening to them"

- Acts 16:25

I love meaning behind the word midnight. It is a transitional term that signifies the ending of the darkest moment and the beginning of a new day. Midnight is literally the turning point of events. It can seem like rock bottom at times but rock bottom can be the best place to welcome the dawn of a new beginning.

Sometimes the dreams we pursue aren't overnight successes. The process may start at midnight, but it seem like visible breakthrough is nowhere to be found. Some people allow this to break them and give up right before it happens.

Change your outlook. The darkest moments in your life can become the most fruitful, depending on how you use them. Take that time and space to eliminate distractions and hear from God. Every moment you spend in a silent place, just you and God, is a moment that brings you closer to clarity, peace and resolve needed to handle the change that occurs at midnight.

Sometimes prayer "at" midnight just isn't enough

but prayer "through" midnight will carry you right to the things you are praying for.

Strength Statement

I will not be afraid to step forward because I'm in a dark season. I will not procrastinate. I will pray and keep it moving.
I know God will meet me!

GOD HEARS

/gäd hirz/

"The Lord is far from the wicked, but he hears the prayer of the righteous."

- Proverbs 15:29

Have you ever taken a demanding course in school with that one instructor that prides his/her self on giving the hardest test on campus? One of the most strictly enforced rules was, "no talking during the test". Think about it. It's unheard of for a student to ask the teacher a question in the middle of an exam and receive an answer.

The same applies in life. If you don't hear anything from God while you are in a difficult situation, just remember He's like a good instructor. He won't answer when we want, but He will refer you to what you've learned in your textbook, His Word.

When Gods hears you it doesn't matter who else ignores you. You may not hear Him during your situation, but remember He's already spoken everything you need to overcome.

Strength Statement

Today, I decide to wake and put more focus on God instead of life's difficult lessons. Not because they don't exist but why worry about a problem I've asked Him to solve. I know He hears me and He's working it out.

VAL·LEYS

/'va-lēz/

MORNING

MOTIVATION

EVERYTHING IN YOUR LIFE THAT'S
BEAUTIFUL ISNT FRUITFUL
BEWARE OF THE DANDELIONS.

"I will open rivers in high places, and fountains in the midst of the valleys: I will make the wilderness a pool of water, and the dry land springs of water."

- Isaiah 41:18

I'm not one of those Christians that will feed you the lie that the day you decide to change your life there would only be good days. You'll have no more obstacles, no more problems or difficult decisions to make. I would be lying to you if I said that because life will present valleys. There will be dark days. There will be things you experience and you don't really know why.

But the key to succeeding in the valleys of life is not denial of their reality but developing a plan of action to overcome them.

In Isaiah 41:18 we see that God is aware that we will go through valleys and low periods that could be detrimental to us. Not only is He aware, but He lets us know He will be with us in the midst of them. The implication of this philosophy is incredible. It means that with God your businesses thrive during periods of recession; you can invest into ideas that everyone tried and failed but have favor there..

Strength Statement

My valley is not a place of destruction
but a place of development. It is a
place of growth and grace.

FO•CUS

/'fəʊkəs/

"Set your minds on things that are above, not on things that are on earth."

- Colossians 3:2

You cannot find God in the midst of trouble when your focus is on the failure. If you are busy examining the condition of your problems, it will be difficult for you to even see when Jesus stretches out his hand towards you. I have discovered that three things really helped me recover from setbacks in life.

1. Address the Fear: The first step I took when I found myself becoming overwhelmed by the troubles in my life was to address the fear that failed me.

The root of all failure lies in fear, and I knew there was something I was afraid of which would keep me from moving forward if I did not address it. You might be afraid of failure itself, or of looking like a fool, or of disappointing those who are looking up to you. Identifying what you fear most and examining it head-on is a huge key to adjusting your focus because you need to know what you're adjusting from.

2. Eliminate destructive habits: We sometimes make use of destructive habits to take our minds off what we are going through but the result of this is usually worse than if we had focused on the problem anyway. Taking drugs or trying to drown your problems in alcohol and sex will only create more

problems for you.

3. Alter your focus: After identifying what you need to turn your focus from, you can now look to God to help you out of that situation.

A lot of times we go through situations and we feel stuck because our focus isn't on the right thing. One of the few things I was able to retain from my overpriced drivers education class was how to avoid accidents while driving. I was taught that the object was not to look to the left or the right lane but find an object straight ahead and focus on the road. If we apply this elementary driving lesson when navigating the ever-winding roads of life, we will understand that nothing else matters but what is ahead.

MORNING

MOTIVATION

PRAYER IS LIKE A VITAMIN FOR OUR
SPIRITUAL IMMUNE SYSTEM.
DON'T LIMIT IT'S PURPOSE TO
THE PAINFUL THINGS. IT'S RECOMMENDED
FOR **DAILY** USE.

THINK

/θɪŋk/

"*Finally, brothers, whatever is true, whatever is honorable, whatever is just, whatever is pure, whatever is lovely, whatever is commendable, if there is any excellence, if there is anything worthy of praise, think about these things.*"

-,Philippians 4:8

We talked about changing your focus yesterday and we are continuing in that line of thought today. Some of you might have been wondering, how exactly do I shift my focus? Not only do you have to shift your focus but you have to alter your mindset and change your way of thinking. In actual fact, altering your way of thinking is how you change your focus.

Negative thoughts create negative outcomes. If you believe that you can't, then you probably can't. Whether you believe it or not, your life is governed by this law. Whatever you think about all the time, whether consciously or subconsciously is a fuel for what you are experiencing in your life. It is like the laws we discussed a few days ago. Even if you do not believe in the law of gravity you will definitely fall to your death if you jump from a skyscraper. Some people think it's the other way around, that what you are experiencing determines what you think about. Allow me to present a different view to you today. The reason why you are experiencing setbacks and failure in your life today is because you were born into a fallen world through parents who also had the sin nature in them. As your parents brought you up, they projected their fears and mindset onto you while teaching you their values too. So therefore, if you have never taken charge of your thinking then you are just living out the life your parents molded into your mind. There's a certain mindset that winners have. Most successful athletes and entrepreneurs will tell you that they eat, sleep and dream about winning because victory first starts in the mind. It is almost impossible for any man to succeed if he is already convinced that he is a failure. People that create wonderful inventions, first of all, have to imagine these things in their heads before they could ever bring them into the physical realm.

Sometimes the things we think about are not necessarily negative, but they are still limiting in their own ways. For example, using the people around you as your standard and measuring how successful you are by how successful your neighbors are is a mediocre mindset that is detrimental to greatness. In order to live a victorious life, you will really need to break out of that box and allow yourself to dare and believe that you can achieve greatness regardless of your present circumstances.

It is not enough to stop thinking wrong thoughts, in order to become significant you will need to pick and choose what you allow yourself to meditate on very carefully. Paul gave us a template in Phil 4:8 where he tells us to think on things that are true, honorable, just, pure, lovely, commendable, excellent and praiseworthy. God has given us standards in His holy word that will help us to be able to discern between good and evil. He has also given us the Holy Spirit who dwells within us and will let us know when our thoughts are straying into the wrong areas.

The moment you convince your natural mind of what is possible, it becomes possible in the spiritual realm. The moment it becomes possible in the spirit realm, God brings it to manifestation.

The Bible says that,

"Whatever you bind on earth will be bound in heaven and whatever you loose on earth will be loosed in heaven".

- Matthew 18:18

There is an interesting translation of that text which I would like to reference for our consideration.

"Whatever you imprison, God will imprison. And whatever you set free, God will set free"

That is why you must allow yourself to be set free of "Stinkin' Thinkin"' or the art of self-sabotage. Whatever you think upon grows and some of us let our thinking drive a wedge between us

and our blessings. So what is the
antidote?
"Let this mind be in you, which was
also in Christ Jesus"
Your life will go in the direction of the
most dominant thoughts in your head.

Strength Statement

Today I will change my life by changing
my thinking, even if the things around
me don't change.

ORDINARY

/ôrdnˌerē/

MORNING

MOTIVATION

INSTEAD OF DEEMING IT A HOPELESS
SEASON OF WAITING
DEVELOP YOURSELF & REFINE YOUR VISON
ALLOW THE SEEDS YOU PLANTED
TIME TO TAKE ROOT.

"When they saw the courage of Peter and John and realized that they were unschooled, ordinary men, they were astonished and they took note that these men had been with Jesus."

- Acts 4:13

The beauty of the bible is that we get the opportunity to read about so many amazing people that have done some amazing things. Sometimes we lose sight of the fact that although these individuals were called by God, they were real people. Real people, with real problems but the one thing that reaming constant was the presence of a real God.

Even if you're born to do something, you still have to be built to handle it.

We must never get to a point in our daily walk with God that we discredit our dependence on God in our lives. Lets be real. He's the primary reason that ordinary people do extraordinary things.

I love the story in the Bible about the boy with the 2 fish and five loaves because we see an ordinary boy, with an ordinary lunch, become a catalyst for an extraordinary miracle.

We know about The Moses
The Elijahs,
The Marys,
The Esters,
The Pauls and Peters

We know about them and should be

encouraged by theirs sorties. But God doesn't love them more than He loves you. Despite setbacks and adversity you still have a purpose and you still have a destiny.

Strength Statement

My life has value. I will enjoy each moment and release insecurity. Today I will be present, not preoccupied.

I'll stop drowning under the weight of "what ifs" by resting in the spontaneity of Jesus.

GOD CHASER

/gäd/ 'CHāsər/

Your Proximity to God will determine your Progression in life. The closer you get to God the more you will begin to see His glory reveled. There is a story in the bible of a man with radical faith named Peter. His greatest desire was to be with Jesus in any way possible.

In the account of Jesus walking on water, we see that the disciples are out to sea and there is a great storm that is around them. The disciples were in, what I like to call, a pregnant moment.

They were facing a storm but also nearing a life changing experience with Jesus. The fascinating thing about this story is that Peter was so determined to get to Jesus that he never let the wind and the waves (Natural things) distract him from his mission. Our desire for

God must match our desire for the things of the word. I love the simplicity of the scripture that says, "If we seek him 1st the things we want or pray for, He will provide". That's an amazing principal to live by because if we chase Him and the material things in our life are taken away or if relationships betray us, and careers lets us down, we will always have enough to start over.

Strength Statement

I will obey the King and ignore the Critics.

HOW ?

/hou/

The backdrop for today's entry involves the study of a colorful interview with Sway Calloway, (host of Sway in the morning), a popular XM radio show and rapper Kanye West. Now before I lose you, let me preface this introduction with my reasoning. My goal is simply to bring practical situations from things we're exposed to (today's challenges) in efforts to resolve future setbacks.

We can't fight today's war with weapons of the past.

With that being said.........this interview included a very typical "Kanye Moment" where he voiced his extreme confidence in himself and his ideas to change to world with his creativity. The climax of this rant was sparked when Sway attempting to give Kanye his 2 cents on how he should accomplish his goals. Sway's attempt clearly aggravated him.... For starters, Sway doesn't have the level of success in the area he was attempting to advise. Stop letting people that were never assigned to your life discourage you. Your destiny is too expensive to let someone control it with their negativity. Secondly, Sway had limitations on what he thought was possible for the rapper to achieve. The greatest enemy to limit the power of God flowing through your life is limiting yourself to your own understanding and expectations of others. The historic rant ended with the very infamous sound bite "You ain't got the answers Sway"

My purpose is not to give you a hip

hop lecture or even defend Kanye but I did want to arrest your attention and affirm a very important truth. WE DON'T HAVE THE ANSWERS!!!!!! The moment that we understand that we can't think our way, plan our way out or pay our way out is the moment we allow God to perform His role as the author and finisher.

Strength Statement

I may not have the answers right now
but I will treat the process with the
same respect as the finished product.
All things do work together.

LOVE

/ləv/

We live in a unique time where hate and negativity generate more buzz than love, but it's extremely important to never let someone or something change your opinion of love. Our goal is to maintain our ability to love in the face of life's deepest hurt and pains without becoming damaged or expectant of disappointment. The goal should always be to remain strong enough to forgive a person for anything, and wise enough to know when to walk away. I'll be the 1st to admit that nothing hurts more than heartbreak. However, heartbreak, I've discovered is like surgery. It's sometimes, painful but always necessary. Allow yourself to see purpose behind procedure. It's easy to get caught up in the images we see of love from celebrities and even among you on social media but create your own love story. It may not be the typical storybook love but real love comes in so many different shapes and sizes. Don't force it. Let love grow organically. It changes everything. Love without fear allows you to appreciate the unexpected.

Strength Statement

Today is a GREAT day to let your fear die and true love live!

MORNING

MOTIVATION

LOVE ON THE PEOPLE YOU DO LIFE WITH
DAILY
IT ONLY TAKES ONE TEXT OR CALL
TO CHANGE SOMEONE'S ENTIRE DAY.

CREATE

/krēˈāt/

At the top of the year I really started to find my groove and boy did I enjoy the freedom it brought. I wasn't trying to copy anyone's path. I was clear and confident in God's plan for my life and self-aware of the things He purposed me to do. When you follow your heart and trust God, the possibilities become endless. It leads you to a moment where you find your lane and accelerate in it. There are so many areas that we as believers can create. Think outside the box be an advocate for balance among other believers. Encourage mental and physical wellness, embrace arts, media and fashion. Change what you've seen. There's no limit to what you can impact. Don't be afraid to purse it. It might be the very thing that sets you free. Be careful though. Idea generation is dope but idea execution is where dreams become reality.

God isn't gonna say..

"Well strategized thy good and faithful servant" or "well planned", He says, "well Done". Today is the day. Just start. Be consistent. Be fearlessly authentic.

Strength Statement

Challenge the status quo, push innovation and refuse to be average. Don't be afraid to do it differently!!!

You Are 1/1

MORNING

MOTIVATION

3 STEP GUIDE TO CONQUER THE DAY
(PRAY +PLAN & PURSUE)

REDIRECT

/rēdrectkt/

I thank God for every closed door, roadblock and detour that protected me from the places not meant for me. The goal is to go through this world and all its challenges without making you bitter or cold but stronger, wiser and more loving. The one thing I loved about my GPS, although is has totally disabled my sense of direction, is a feature that has saved me more time and frustration. This feature is powered by a satellite located thousands of miles above us that can trace our location. This is good news because no matter how bad things get along the journey, someone up above has a different perspective. Don't let the fear of taking the wrong steps and choosing the wrong relationships stop you.

Corrections provide opportunities to work. God is not only the God of the destination but He's the God of the detour.

Strength Statement

Direction > Speed - Focus on moving
with purpose today not pace.

#ProgressNotPerfection

Sometimes difficult roads lead to
beautiful destinations. The journey is
just preparation!

WIN TODAY

/win/ /ty'win

Today! Fresh start, blank canvas. Take this moment to thank God that everything you faced every month until now didn't destroy you. Start speaking blessings over your day. Start setting goals, spiritually and financially. Don't be complacent. You've got this. Expect better. Aim to please God more today. Approach it differently, reposition your priorities and remember why you started.

Step up your game plan at work, school and in your relationships.

Don't fast forward to tomorrow just yet, use this moment to build momentum and seek clarity. This is your daily reminder that you can handle anything tomorrow throws at you.

Strength Statement

Today is won because Jesus is constant. His grace is constant. His loves is constant. His plan is constant. Circumstances change, Jesus does not.

STRENGTHEN

/streNG(k)THtem

"Wake up! Strengthen what remains and is about to die, for I have found your deeds unfinished in the sight of my God."

- Rev 3:2

The stretching of your muscles builds strength. Have you ever been to the gym and done any type of weight training? Well, more often you leave feeling worse than when you came in. What an interesting dynamic. The same motion and method we use to build strength causes initial pain. The purpose of resistance training is to cause muscle damage or "positive damage". The immediate result of that damage causes weakness, but over time your muscles actually begin to repair and regrow, preparing you to be able to handle future damage while experiencing less pain. Everything life hits us with is a part of our own unique strengthening process. Some days will be easier than others but remember the bad days can be used to reveal a deficiency or an area of opportunity we shouldn't ignore. Your circle of influence will be vital in this journey of recovering strength. Audit your circle. Include a few people within your circle that are stronger than you, financially or spiritually and mentally. Force yourself to raise the bar on your expectations.

Strength Statement

God is not done. Today is not the end of your story. Embrace this chapter. Trust the author. What you see now is not the ending!